**BLACKHEATH DAWN**
**LIMITED**

## Published by Blackheath Dawn Limited 2014

## All rights reserved.

Blackheath Dawn Ltd.

Georgian house. The Thoroughfare, Halesworth. Suffolk. IP19 8AP

Email: Info@Blackheathdawn.co.uk

Len Biddlecombe has asserted his moral right to be identified as the author of Life of Love

For more information on the author,
http://Blackheathdawnwriters.co.uk/lenbiddlecombe

---

This book of Poetry is a personal tribute to my beloved wife Barbara. It serves as a constant reminder of my undying devotion towards her throughout our long married life.


Over the years I have written many poems and sonnets to her, these are just a few that have survived the passage of time.
There is only so much one can write in the way of loving words and it is unavoidable that some phrases and expressions are often repeated. This should take nothing away from the seriousness and honest meaning of my deep love for her and everything she has done for me over all the years it has been my pleasure to know her, both as my girlfriend and my wife. No words can ever express exactly what she means to me however these words have enabled me to convey, in some small way the deep love and devotion I will always have for her.


I love you Barb with all my heart,
Your loving husband,

Len.    XX.

# Life of Love

For Barbara

## Len Biddlecombe

# Table of contents

# 1966.

This was a poem to remember our first real time spent together for a few days at Yarmouth in a caravan. This was perhaps one of our happiest times and a never to be forgotten period as we got to know each other. This was soon to be followed by a holiday in a caravan at nearby Kessingland the following year.

# The early days.

We all went down to Yarmouth Town to a van right near the sea
There was Mr., Mrs. Master Frost, Barb the girls and me.
A lot to fit in you may say, seven in one van,
Snowy didn't think so when he said "Sleep where you can".

The parents took one double bed, the girls had number two
A single bed for Trev and I, we were a motley crew.
We turned in about half past one all quiet and peaceful but
The wind blew in more ways than one and the door would not keep shut!
First sheets sailed off then blankets too to give us all a fright
Sleeping in our night attire we looked a rare old sight.
But soon came daylight, half past six and Snowy's out in force
Charging round to get his kicks up and down the course!
Then a cup of tea in bed, a quick chat and a fag
While Linda nips off to the shops to buy the Sunday rag.
A nice hot breakfast then a shave, a half hour with the ball
Just to make the neighbours rave and drive them up the wall.
A drink or two at dinner time, just half a dozen each
Then back for lunch, a speedy change and all off down the beach.
It's back for tea, some more football then back out on the beer
A little apprehensive now as farewell time draws near
And then at last it's time to go, it's all been such good fun
Until Friday please take care and thanks for all you've done.

# 1967

Such a lovely clubhouse, miles of golden sand
When you hire a caravan down at Kessingland.
Lots of laughs and bags of fun, Bingo every night
Kegs and kegs of Special Mild just to keep you tight!
Eddie on the guitar till it's time for bed
Then off to the caravan to rest your weary head..................BUT
First we have to work it out where can we all sleep,
In the sink? Standing up? Lying in a heap?
For there's just one double bed and that's for mum and dad
Two single beds and four to sleep, it really drives you mad!
"Put the girls together then," says Snowy using sense
"And we'll go in the single beds and Len, there's still the Gents
Or halfway up the chimney, behind the cupboard door,
Underneath the caravan or on the kitchen floor!
Lay him this way so his head is bound to hit the wall,
If he wants to miss the table he must roll up in a ball!"
Gradually we settle down, and then Linda starts to roll
She gets turned out to sleep elsewhere and ends up in the bowl!
Then Tricia starts to twist and shout, it's not the urge she's got,
She's settled down to spend the night, balanced on a knot!
With Barbara getting tossed around by arms and legs and bums
Snatching little bits of sleep till the morning comes.
Then there's Snowy up and out to make a pot of tea
He washes up and wanders round and treads all over me!
It's really lovely getting up and putting on your togs
To leap out in the morning air, it's raining cats and dogs!
I'm so glad that I could go and share your holiday,

Kessingland's the place to go but NOT the place to stay!!
After the excitement of a couple of carefree holidays together it was back to reality and down to earth again.

The following effort was written after I returned home, leaving the Frost family to enjoy what was left of their annual break. It illustrates just how much I was missing them all and especially my darling Barbara.

# I think of you.

A sausage roll, a pinch of snuff, a cup of lukewarm tea,
A jar of Brylcream in the sun, a catapult, a flea,
An apple hanging from a tree, a badly worn out shoe,
A chestnut and a garden pea all make me think of you.
From when my feet are freezing cold to when my pulses race,
On meeting someone very old I see your smiling face!
You think perhaps the cheek of it comparing me with these,
Now calm yourself, don't have a fit, listen to me please.
The answer is I think of you with everything I see,
The good things and the bad ones too, you're all the world to me.

# The one I love.

The stillness of the evening air, the twinkling stars above
Remind me just how much I care for the girl I love.
Each time I feel a gentle breeze my thoughts are just the same,
It seems to murmur through the trees just whispering your name.
The rippling of a country stream through meadows bathed in sun
Conjures many a blissful dream of my favourite one.
Watching falling autumn leaves drifting from above,

Every moment my heart grieves for the one I love.
When the world is bathed in green, the happiness of spring,
Everywhere new life is seen and all the songbirds sing.
Every beauty God has given for us all to share,
Be it Earth or be it Heaven never will compare
To the girl who won my heart and the entire world must know
Barbara we will never part for I love you so.

These poems are designed to show my deep affection at a time when our circumstances were such that we desperately needed all the support we could give each other. Then we got our freedom and were married.

## How much

You know how much I love you; you know how much I care
You know how much it means to me to know you're always there.
Perhaps I really should have said you think you know, you see
I don't think you realise you're everything to me.
Your smiling face your lovely form, the wondrous things you do,
There are a thousand reasons why I'm in love with you
And I will always love you because my Barb you see
I'm yours today and everyday throughout eternity
And now we've made our wedding vows and you've become my wife,
I pledge myself to you alone throughout our married life.
Whatever lies before us, whatever we must bear,
We will face together, the good and bad we'll share,
For today I've taken a really lovely bride
Whatever life may throw at us I'll be by your side.

Len Biddlecombe writes 'There are times in life when certain experiences stand out for ever in ones memory. One is surely the moment when a man and his partner hold their firstborn child for the very first time. 'Life's most precious moment' tries to reproduce the joy shared when couples become parents. It is a moment in time that can only be appreciated when two people actually experience it.

I enjoyed writing 'Life's most precious moment' as it brought back my own special memory from many years ago. Of all the poems I've written this one holds a special meaning for me'.

# Life's most precious moment

It's life's most precious moment between a man and his wife,

When they are together and produce their first new life.

It often starts when he's asleep at 3 a.m. or so,

She wakes her weary partner and says 'It's time to go.'

Her bag is packed and ready; they've rehearsed it all before.

There's no need to panic, but he does and that's for sure!

A quick drive to the hospital, there won't be long to wait,

If only he could keep awake it really would be great.

Everything is ready, no need to induce;

Contractions getting regular, she's ready to produce.

Suffering hours of labour she screams out in pain,

'I'll never let you put me through all this again.'

You hold her hand so tightly but she grips you like a vice.

Caesarean is called for, Oh God it isn't nice.

But now you hold your baby, you and proud mum there,

It is Life's most precious moment, each of you can share.

This next piece illustrates Len's humour.

# A Wife.

When I was young and carefree life was full of fun
I went anywhere I liked, with almost anyone.
Went to clubs and pubs and bars when I was in my teens
Smoked and drank, wore tee shirts, leather coats and jeans.
Going with a different girl almost every day
Until the girl got serious, then I was on my way.
When I grew to manhood I began to understand
To become successful, you need a helping hand.
I became more sensible, took a grip on life
Finished all my crazy ways and took myself a wife.
My happiness is now complete and when I wake each day
To find her there beside me, I turn to her and say
'I really love you darling and everything you do
Life would be worth nothing if I did not have you.'
I couldn't face the future without you being there,
I can't say you are beautiful but you are a millionaire!!

It became a tradition for me to concoct a poem for Barb each time her birthday came round. This was taken a step further when our wedding anniversary arrived each year on 3$^{rd}$. February so at least two poems a year were required. Inevitably there became sameness to the themes and many of them were similar in terms of endearment. The following efforts are a selection written on these occasions.

# Birthdays and Anniversaries.

Once again your birthday's here, how quickly, yet another year,
At the risk of sounding rotten, at our age they're best forgotten!
But I can never forget you for all the wondrous things you do.
Without you I'd have a sorry life, to me you are a marvelous wife
And nothing is too good or dear to give you, but we're broke I fear
So there's very little I can say except I hope you have a happy day
With deepest love from me to you, now back to work there's a load to do!

We can never stop the years as they go rolling by,
One thing nothing can prevent is that I'll love you till I die.
The 3$^{rd}$. of Feb.'s a special day, a day we made our own,
But darling each and every day my love is yours alone.
Although the years may come and go, I know we'll never part
For I want and need you so and love you with all my heart.

# My love.

When I was young I used to dream
Of Candy Floss and pink ice cream.
I thought the world was full of fun
And happiness for everyone.

Without a worry or a care
With pleasures for us all to share.
All too soon I grew to know
Problems face us as we grow,

Decisions that we all must make
Directions each one has to take.
About this time I fell in love,
Held hands beneath the stars above.

This lovely girl transformed my life
When she agreed to be my wife.
How wonderful this life can be
Now she'll do anything for me.

My fears are really at an end
For she is now my greatest friend.
Once more I can enjoy my life
I have a soul mate and a wife.

# Losing a loved one.

I feel I've been so lucky for I've have never been alone
Unlike so many sorry folk who face life on their own.
They've lost a son or daughter, a husband or a wife
Because of some disaster that has wrecked their life.
We feel we want to help them, alas what can we do
It's difficult to understand just what they're going through.
How can they recover to live their life again?
How can we assist them to overcome their pain?
Perhaps we can persuade them that life's not always sad
There are many rich and lovely things to share among the bad
We cannot turn the clock back or change a tragedy
Life can be so very cruel but what will be, will be
No one can touch our memories they're ours for evermore
To treasure and to cherish of happy times before
So honouring their memory we put aside our strife,
To look towards the future and to rebuild our life.
We know we owe it to them to overcome our tears
And restore some happiness to our remaining years
We never will forget them not even for a day
Knowing we will meet again somewhere along the way

# When times are hard

When times are rough and rocky it's hard work just to smile.
Sometimes it's been you alone, who've made it all worthwhile,
But one thing I will never lose whatever they may do
Is the never-ending love I have my darling Barb for you.
So when I say "I love you, happy anniversary"
Remember what I really mean, "You mean the world to me."

## 1991

I wonder where I would have been if I had not met you.
Would I be rich and happy or maybe poor and blue?
Would I come in every night a smile upon my face?
Would I live with someone else in some far off place?
No one can turn the clock back, no one can really tell
But twenty-three years ago today I think I did real well!
And as the years have tumbled by we've laughed at times and cried
Yet all the time through thick and thin you've been here by my side.
If I could live my life again I wouldn't change a thing,
I love you when I'm feeling down for all the joy you bring.
Raise your glass; let's say a toast for all that's gone before
To a happy anniversary and many, many more
For I love you my darling and we will never part,
You mean the very world to me I love you with all my heart.

# And in September……………..

Happy birthday darling, you mean the world to me,
I'll love you with all my heart throughout eternity.


# 1992.


This card is really full of words so it would seem this time
There isn't really any need for my usual loving rhyme………..HOWEVER
You may be disappointed so, to satisfy your fears
I'll say just a word or two about twenty-four long years.
For that's how long it is today since you became my wife,
But really you're much more than that, for you've become my life.
I can't imagine what I'd do if we should ever part,
You mean the very world to me; I love you with all my heart
And as the years go tumbling by and old age comes our way
I only pray you're by my side through each and every day
For I just can't explain in words how much you mean to me
And how I'll love you ever more throughout eternity.

# Again in September 1992...............

Hello, I hope you're feeling great!

**Birthdays were such happy times when we were young and gay,**
**They don't seem so important now we are old and grey.**
**We just want to ignore them, forget when they are due**
**And as you know I love you that's just what we will do,**
**I won't give you a present, no meal to celebrate,**
**Just a card to say "Hello, I hope you're feeling great."**

**(I did though!)**

1993 was a very special year, heralding as it did our Silver Wedding Anniversary and it called for a very special dedication to my darling wife, here it is.

# Silver Wedding

**A quarter of a century, two and a half decades,**
**Surely feelings tarnish, surely true love fades.**
**There must be temptation to fancy other charms,**
**To share a night of passion in someone else's arms.**
**With some no doubt it happens every time they can**
**But not with me my darling, I'm a one-girl man.**

# Ten thousand days

Ten thousand days we've been together and all that we dreamed of
Has now come true for we have shared a lifetime of true love.
I'm so proud of our children; we've watched our two boys grow
To two fine men and on the way we had some fun you know
And now we have our daughter, pleasures will not cease,
She's a copy of your loveliness, our beautiful Denise.

As the years keep passing by and we are growing old,
My love for you will never fade though passion may grow cold
And when our days are over and earthly pleasures through,
I only ask that I can share eternity with you,
For in the life hereafter, whatever it may be,
I will not fear for anything as long as you're with me.

Enough of thoughts of sadness, of worries and of fears
For we are celebrating our twenty-five great years.
The hard times and the good times, the grey skies and the blue,
Nothing ever mattered as long as I had you.
So let's have smiles and laughter and make all sadness go,
Just let me hold and kiss you for Barb, I love you so.

# 1994.

Another year, another card, another little rhyme,
There's one thing we can never stop, the march of Father Time.
To think that we've been married for twenty-six long years,
We've watched our family growing up, shared happy times and tears
And yet if I could start again I wouldn't change a thing
Except, I'd pawn my satchel to buy your wedding ring!
Then we'd have spent longer still living side by side.
I'd dearly love to have made you my blushing teenage bride!
But let's not try to change the past; it hasn't been so bad,
We could fill up many books with the lovely times we've had.
And even on our darker days, when we're feeling blue
I thank God for my greatest gift, the love I share with you.
Whatever perils lie ahead in our twilight years of life
I'll never want for anything with you Barb as my wife,
We may not have Champagne my love, or Caviar, or wealth
But raise your glass of Guinness, and toast to our good health.
Tear up the bills just for today let the celebrations start
For you mean the entire world to me, I love you with all my heart.

# September 7th. 1994.

Happy Birthday dearest Barb, how many? Fifty-two?
Seems you're knocking on a bit but come now don't feel blue.
With your family all around you and a helping hand from me
There really is no reason you can't manage fifty-three!
Seriously Barb I love you more and more each day,
You mean the very world to me in each and every way.
And as our birthdays come and go it only proves to me
I'll never be without you throughout eternity.
So darling please enjoy today and each day through your life,
A very happy birthday my young and lovely wife.

# 1995.

Barb, you know I love you and all you mean to me
Even though you've reached the ripe old age of fifty-three!
Seriously, you're wonderful in each and every way
It seems you're looking younger and lovelier each day.
I really can't imagine why such a thing should be
Perhaps it is contentment because you married me!
No matter what the reason it pleases me to say
Have a really super smashing time, a wonderful birthday.

This next poem could have been written at any time during our married life, it is perhaps the most moving one I have ever written. I think it was put together somewhere around this period though it is timeless and remains true to this day. Fifty lines long it reflects our feelings for each other as we reach the later stages of our married life together and highlights the problems every couple have to face as they move from middle to old age.

# Life and death.

Life is just an interlude, a moment so sublime,
A flash of sparkling sunshine in the dark abyss of time.
We know not where we come from or where we have to go
Our fleeting years of living are the only joys we know.
Giving help to others, always glad to share
All life's little pleasures, showing that we care.

We love and help our children through their early years,
Join them in their laughter, wipe away their tears,
But we deserve our pleasures for all we try to do,
My life really started the day that I met you.
I said "We'll not be parted, not even for a day,"
But now the years have passed us by and death will have its way.

Time is overtaking us although it breaks my heart
I know one day the day will dawn when you and I must part.
Not by choice you understand, I'd never want to go
Because you mean the world to me and I love you so.
But when I have to leave you on that God forsaken day
Dry your tears, remember I'm never far away.

On a winters evening in blinding driving snow,
If you listen carefully you'll hear me say "Hello"
I'll whisper that I love you clear above the storm
Telling you "Be careful, make sure you wrap up warm."
And when it comes to springtime those balmy breezes sigh
Gently through the treetops you'll hear me whisper "Hi"

Sit out in the garden like we used to do,
Although you cannot see me I'll spend an hour with you."
Then in the heat of summer with windows open wide
I'll murmur that you're beautiful as I settle by your side.
I'll watch your lovely body as you're soaking up the sun
Remembering our happy years until each day is done.

In autumn in the garden as leaves fall from the tree
Listen to the gentle breeze and surely you'll hear me
Saying "Darling, do not mourn me, do not fret or cry,
For I am always with you until the day you die."
You never need be frightened, hold up your head with pride,
Whatever ills befall you I'll be there at your side.

Although you cannot see me you needn't have a care,
I never will desert you; you'll know I'm always there.
For you to me were everything throughout our married life
A happy trusting partner, a truly loving wife.
Someone whose stunning beauty that captivated me
Should pledge your true undying love for everyone to see.

A mother to our children, you cared and loved them so,
A person so devoted that I was proud to know.
My memories untarnished I'll treasure on and on
Forever, in my heart of hearts although my life has gone,
And I will never really rest until that final day
When you leave this world behind and come to me and say,

"We are now together, no more pain to bear,
We'll wander through the halls of time, paradise we'll share.

# Around 1997.

It's easy to write poetry when things are going fine,
The words just seem to slot in place so well, line after line.
There are so many things to say, so many ways to tell
Yes writing poems is easy when all is going well,
But writing poems is harder when things are going wrong,
The words just seem to linger, the lines all seem too long.
I think that also sums up life, it's easy when you share
A happy life that's trouble free with never a single care,
But when you have a hard life with problems you must bear
Then you need someone to love, someone to really care.
For many years, yes twenty-nine we've had to struggle on
With sometimes just each other to heap our problems on,
And on this day so precious whatever else I do
I know that I must make it clear just how much I love you,
Although it's not been easy to get along the way
I will always love you, forever, every day.
Nobody can change it whatever they may do
I will always love you Barb, my darling I love you.

# A Bank

If bad luck Barb befalls me, a stroke or heart attack
Or maybe a road accident from which I can't come back,
Or any other sudden act causing me to die
Without a chance to see you and say our last "Goodbye"
Just look in my chest of drawers, in the fourth drawer down,
The one I keep my gloves in underneath two pairs of brown,
You'll see a "Tootal" plastic box with a pale blue frilly bow
Inside, look underneath it, there's something you should know
Together with a present I've saved up for this day
I'd far rather be here with you but it'll help you pay your way.
Don't be afraid to spend it, go on a spending spree
Enjoy all life's great pleasures but spare a thought for me!

# 1997

Now you're knocking on a bit, what is it, fifty-five?
There have been some subtle changes but at least you're still alive!
Some humps and bumps here and there, rheumatics, so they say,
A line or two on your face, your hair has streaks of grey,
Some extra weight down below though nothing seems to flop.
Some inches round the middle, a bit of spread up top.
You used to be a figure eight, a really perfect mix,
You've retained your figure though it's now more like a six!
Seriously, I love to bait you just to see you smile,
I think you carry your age well with beauty, poise and style,
And anyway it matters not whatever shape you'll be
For you know I worship you, you're everything to me,
So don't let's count the birthdays, it's you that I adore
A happy birthday darling and many, many more.

# 1998.

We've reached another landmark in our married life,
For thirty years ago today you became my wife.
We've faced life's many problems, the good times and the bad
And I remember vividly the happy times we've had.
We've never had much money but then again who cares,
You never know, this time next year we may be millionaires!
And even if, by some chance this dream may not come true,
I'm still the richest man alive as long as I've got you.
I remember thirty years ago when we were "boy and girl"

And on this anniversary you really are my "pearl."
I may not go to heaven but for what it's worth
I'm sure as long as I've got you my heaven's here on earth.
And when the candles flicker and my time here is through,
My only prayer will be to share eternity with you.

# 1999.

Ecstasy and sorrow, joyfulness and tears
We've been through so many things in thirty-one long years.
Tragedy, calamity, happiness, delight,
Days of blinding sunshine, the darkest hours of night
Nothing could defeat us as we've stood side by side,
Sometimes we've shared laughter other times we've cried.
It never has been easy but we have journeyed on
Sharing life's emotions our love was always strong
And now that we've grown older I'm proud that you're my wife
There's no one else I want to share the twilight years of life.
My love for you is boundless, I treasure every day
That we can spend together and every night I pray
A prayer of deepest gratitude for everything you do,
A prayer of loving thankfulness for the day that I met you,
And as we share our feelings I'll always try to show
My passion and devotion because I love you so
And we'll go on together no matter what may be,
Whatever life may throw at us we'll master it, you'll see,
Enjoy our anniversary and roll on thirty-two and three,
I love you Barb my darling, you're the entire world to me.

# 21st. Century.

## 3rd. February 2000.

Another card another year, my how time does fly,
We just can't seem to slow it down no matter how we try.
Another anniversary for you and me to share,
Another opportunity to show how much I care.
For as the years go rushing by one thing comes shining through,
The most important thing I have is my deep love for you.
It somehow seems so natural, so right in every way
For us to be together each night and every day.
Of course we have our arguments, every couple do,
But nothing that could interfere with the way that I love you.
We've shared most of our lifetime good memories and bad,
No one could imagine the experiences we've had.
We've struggled through misfortunes, enjoyed our pleasures too
Nothing life could throw at us could split up me and you.
We've had and raised our family they stand out in a crowd
They've grown up into fine adults, no wonder we feel proud.
But now the years have passed us by no longer young and gay
We now prefer to share our time in a more retiring way.
There's only one thing that I need to help me struggle through
Whatever problems lie ahead and that, dear Barb is you!

# 7th. September 2000.

No poem in your birthday card I've not a thing to say
Except, I love you dearly, have a lovely time today.
Oh, and by the way some other poems will surely come your way
And I'll give you your present much later in the day.

# 2001, February 3rd.

Love is like a red, red rose which grows each summer's day.
Regretfully it isn't true I'm very sad to say.
The rose can only bloom in spring when sunny days are here,
My love for you is shining bright each day of every year.
Twelve thousand and fifty-three long days, that's thirty-three long years
We've shared each hour together through happiness and tears.
Three lovely children we've produced each filling us with pride,
Tonight it's great to have them here their partners by their side,
And now we've reached our twilight years there's one wish to come true,
I want to share forever eternity with you,
For you are such a beauty so lovely to behold
I'm proud to have you by my side if I might be so bold.
A vision of such loveliness for everyone to see
I can't believe you'd ever want to share your life with me.
So darling Barb I want to say you're all the world to me
I love you with all my heart, happy anniversary.

# September 7th. 2001.

Another birthday comes around; you're fifty-nine today!
No time for celebrations with sixties on the way,
Insurance Companies sending you their latest pension plan,
Take out a funeral cover scheme right now, while you can!

They seem to want to join with you and help you celebrate
As long as you insure with them before it is too late!
So have a grin and bear it Barb, dismiss it from your mind
Enjoy life's greatest pleasures of each and every kind.

You know how much I love you; I've told you every year,
It never will diminish, of that you need not fear.
We're growing old together, partners on life's ride
Holding hands so deep in love, always side by side.

So Barb, enjoy your birthday, you're everything to me,
Remember we're an item and evermore will be
So listen to my good advice from one who ought to know
For I weathered all these feelings just four years ago!

# 3rd. February 2002

Another year has passed us by with memories to add
To all the others we possess for years of fun we've had.
Remembering the early days, the pleasures that we shared
We had so little money but neither of us cared.

We didn't go to parties, a very rare night out
Otherwise we stayed at home, love without a doubt.
Holding hands and cuddling while we watched T.V.
Contented in each other's arms, happy as could be.

Then the children came along filling us with pride
Then we faced new problems always side by side
Things were never easy the way they are today,
Washing Machines and Fridges cost more than we could pay.

Dishwashers, Tumble dryers the housewives life is fine,
In our time your pride and joy was the outside washing line!
But we still had our pleasures though simple they would be,
There was always brush and dustpan, the open fire and me!

I marvel at your beauty, Barb, you're lovelier each day,
I'm proud to have you by my side you're great in every way.
I love our nights of passion enjoying all your charms
Lying wrapped together in each other's arms.

But where has our lifetime gone, the years have passed us by.
The wondrous pleasures we have shared together you and I,

How many more are to come? Nobody can say,
I just enjoy you near me every night and day.

So though the time will surely come when you and I must part
They'll never ever split us up; you're always in my heart.
Whatever life may throw at us there's nothing it can do
To erase the lifelong memories and love I have for you.

Our thirty-four years together have been beyond compare,
We've had our joys and heartaches but you've always been there,
So, on our anniversary I am just left to say
Thank you, Barb my darling for this and every day.

# Sands

The sands of time keep running out it's yet another year,
But while we love each other there's nothing we need fear.
Whatever the future holds for us side by side we'll stand
Facing all life's problems together, hand in hand.
A lifetime of devotion over thirty-five long years
Enjoying happy laughter, sharing tragic tears.

Your beauty still astounds me, your loveliness divine,
I find it hard to understand how all this can be mine,
And age will never tarnish the memories we share,
Our love will last forever, a love beyond compare.
Forget about the big six-oh and always understand
You are and you will always be my castle in the sand.

# 2003, our anniversary,

The sands of time keep running out faster every year,
It's time to get the "poem pen" out, our special day is here.
The greatest day of my whole life, I'll not forget the date,
It was the third of February, nineteen sixty-eight.

We made our vows and promises to honour all our life
And on that very special day you became my wife.
Throughout the thirty-five long years I've promised to be true,
I've never been unfaithful or lost my love for you.

We've shared such lovely moments enjoying all life's joys
And in both Dave and Peter we've had two smashing boys.
The coming of our daughter was such a special treat,
She was so sweet and beautiful our marriage was complete

Truly, really all my greatest luck was sharing life with you
For all the things you've done for me my darling I love you.
Even if I fail to celebrate another "special day"
I'll always say I love you Barb in each and in every way.

And thanks for all the love we've known throughout so many years,
There'll be no time for sadness; there'll be no time for tears
Just time to give such grateful thanks for all our married life
To you my dearest darling, my sweet and lovely wife.

To quote the famous words of that local poet you know so
    well……………..

The spirit's strong, the flesh is weak,
The muscles ache, the bones all creak.
The passion's hot, performance cold,
Oh why, Oh why do we grow old!!!

# Birthday number 61,

# 7th. September 2003.

The years roll on relentlessly, another one goes by.
We cannot turn the clock back no matter how we try.
You are extremely lucky Barb, although it's very strange
Despite the years that tarnish me you never seem to change.

A little wrinkle here and there, an extra inch or two,
Just a hint of greying hair, that's all it's done to you.
Your beauty is amazing; it's there for all to see,
Your body is delightful; it still does things to me.

I'll never want another love, you're everything to me
To wake each day beside you is where I want to be.
No one could ever take your place; my love is just for you,
Your loveliness is everywhere in everything you do.


So even though you're sixty-one I want the world to see
That age will never tarnish you, you're seventeen to me!
And if I could sum up my love the one word I would state
To show I love you darling, the word I'd use is GREAT!!

# My Birthday

The year 2003 I had rather an important birthday of my own.

It is the fourth of April Two Thousand and Three,
That's nothing special you may say but it is to me.
It's one date in the calendar that I must celebrate
For I was born on this day in Nineteen Thirty Eight,
A milestone, for that means I'm sixty-five today,
My working life is over or so our laws all say.
I am an old age pensioner, a sad old thing to be,
I prefer retirement, sounding better far to me.

On this very special day my thoughts begin to stray
To several other milestones that happened on the way.
The first was on my birthday, Nineteen Thirty Eight,
My mum was forty-two years old, she left it rather late.
My dad was really blameless, he'd been away you see
Preparing for the second war he had no time for me!
And then a lucky weekend pass, or so I've heard them say,
A short time spent together and I was on the way!

I was seven when it ended in Nineteen Forty Five,

A milestone to remember, we were grateful to survive.
My father, brother, sister all came safely through
Once more we were a family and started life anew.
I went on to Grammar School in Nineteen Forty Nine
And I enjoyed it very much, life was looking fine.
Seventeen years of football for the local team.
But reaching middle thirties I then ran out steam.

I'd joined up with the forces, conscripted I should say
For three years in the R.A.F. right through to demob day.
Now I was nearing twenty-two with lots of things to do
And as I had more leisure time I learned the Guitar too.
I formed a group, The Easybeats, the youngsters all went mad
We played at "Gigs" and weddings and what a time we had!
I tried a few romances but nothing seemed quite right
Then one day I met Barbara and it was love at first sight.

The next milestone was special and really very great,
We married in the February, Nineteen Sixty Eight.
And as our love life blossomed and time kept rolling on,
Another milestone happened with the birth of David John.
Followed by his brother, one December morn,
An early Christmas present, Peter James was born!

Married life was wonderful and so exciting too
Until shortly before Christmas, Nineteen Seventy Two,
Suddenly my father died, I really shed some tears,
We never had been closer than in the last few years.
And then in nineteen Eighty, Barb's dad Snowy died,
A man I had respected since she became my bride.

To complete our sadness, our mums both died too.
We became the Senior Generation, as all couples do.
In August Nineteen Eighty Two the time arrived to stop
Our daughter Denise Jean was born; it was time to "shut up shop!"
David married Alison, Pete and Amanda settled down,
Denise became the Manager of Olan Mills in town

Now quite recently, engaged and settled down with Dean
It is perhaps the greatest period of life we've ever seen.
Grandchildren in Ben and Rhys have joined our happy band,
There's nothing left for us to do as you will understand.
Except to enjoy retirement with all its joys and tears
And hope we stay together for many happy years.
So I hope you will forgive me reminiscing in this way,
But I am now a pensioner, I'm sixty-five today!

# Thirty-sixth Wedding Anniversary

# 3rd. February 2004.

The words have all been said before, the feelings are well known,
They've always been the honest truth as years of love have shown.
But never have they meant as much as they mean today.
I've never found it easier to turn to you and say
That famous simple statement "Barb, I love you so,"
You mean the entire world to me, more than you could know.
And on our Anniversary, thirty-six years wed

There's never been a truer word that I have ever said.

You look after all my needs in every kind of way,
I've enjoyed your company each and every day.
Waking up each morning curled up by your side
Since that day so long ago when you became my bride.
Holding you tight in my arms whispering "I love you"
Before we faced the day ahead and all we had to do.
The problems we have had to face all our married years,
You've always shared my good times and wiped away my tears.

There's never been a moment that I have felt regret
Throughout our life together since the day we met,
And now we've reached our twilight years I can look back and say
Despite the bad times we have shared there's never been a day
That I have ever doubted the love I have for you,
Thank you Barb for all you've done for me our whole life through,
And every little bit of love remaining in my life
Will always be for you Barb, my dearest darling wife.

# BUT

Whatever kind of present can I buy for you?
I've searched the second hand shops, why should I buy "new".
You know I can't afford it no matter how I feel,
I've even had to cancel my arrangements for the meal!

I've been round to the Co-op and brought cheese biscuits back
I know how much you like them and it is a seven pack.
So please don't think that I've been mean, it really isn't true
I almost bought a single pack of Walkers Crisps for you!

But felt that after all these years you deserved much more,
So I will only eat three packs and you deserve the four!
And to prove my love for you my darling never fear
I promise we will have a slap up meal again next year!

I'll be starting to save up from this very day,
Though I fear you'll have to cut down to one Guinness every day!
And with the money that we save next year you'll be full
I'll treat you to a Scampi meal at the old Black Bull!

I think you will be longing for our next Anniversary
Despite the three-pound twenty five it's going to cost me!!

# 62nd Birthday, 7th September 2004.

Every year about this time I like to write a little rhyme
    Telling you I love you so, something you must surely know.
Birthdays are not all the rage when you start to reach our age
    But now that you are sixty-two don't think the fun has gone for you,
Cast off all those birthday blues and get out your old dancing shoes,
    What? You can't get them on your feet, your corns all start to overheat,
Never mind, my knees both ache so dancing may be a mistake!
    Let's sit, I'll hold you in my arms remembering your many charms
I'll try and find the words to say to help to brighten up your day
    There's nothing else I need to do but whisper Barb I do love you.

# 37th Wedding Anniversary

3rd. February 2005.

On Wedding Anniversaries and on your birthdays too
    I love to write a little poem about my love for you.
And as you would imagine now that we've been wed
    For all of thirty- seven years, everything's been said.
However I still wonder how you can look so neat
    Your beauty and your figure so lovely, so complete.
I feel I am so lucky to have a wife like you,
    All I can do is look in awe at everything you do.
Without you I would have no life, no reason to exist
    For every day I spend with you is never to be missed.
Your loveliness astounds me, the funny things you say
    Help to keep me cheerful, every single day.
For what seems like a lifetime, for thirty-seven years
    We have shared such happiness although there have been tears.
We've really been so lucky, the very best of friends
    And passionately deep in love, the story never ends.

Whatever else we have to face, in sun or stormy weather
   I know we'll overcome it while we still pull together.
So on this Anniversary it just remains to say
   Thank you Barb, my darling, for each and every day,
For all our time together, for everything you do
   I'll never find the words to say my darling I love you.
The family said it wouldn't last, that we'd split up somehow,
   Thirty-seven years have gone, what would they all say now!!

# 7th September 2005,

# sixty third birthday.

A very happy birthday Barb, sixty three years old today.
They say you are as old as you feel that makes you seventy I'd say!
Seriously you look so young and carry your age so well
You don't look sixty three today no one would ever tell.
If I could turn the clock back I'd make you twenty one
As long as I could be as young, wouldn't it be fun
Alas we cannot do it, the years keep rolling by
We have to make the most of things and not roll up and die.
So on this very special day I'll thank the lord above
For giving you to share my life and send you all my love
So never ever shed a tear on reaching sixty three
You'll always look like twenty one and full of life to me

.

## 2006, Our thirty eighth wedding anniversary.

Another year has come and gone, the totals thirty eight
It's really rather frightening although I think it's great
We've shared such precious moments since the day we met
I've never ever doubted you such happiness we get
From simply being side by side enjoying togetherness
It's such a wondrous pleasure it's really nothing less
Than facing life and holding hands each and every day
Dealing with life's problems in our own special way.
I wonder where on earth I'd be if I had not met you
You make me feel so happy with everything you do.
So darling on this special day I simply must confess
I love you oh so dearly Barb, take care, good luck, God bless.

# 7th September 2006,

## Your Sixty Fourth birthday.

You've reached the age of sixty four, it must be quite a shock
It's time to stop and meditate, time for taking stock.
Next year you'll be sixty five when everyone retires
It signals time to quieten down your working life expires.
Though in your case you'll carry on I know that it will be
For you will still feel duty bound to take good care of me
Just as you have for all the years since the day we met
You've made my life so special as good as it could get
I bless the day I married you all those years ago
Who could have guessed we'd stick it out no one could ever know
So every year your birthday is an occasion I admire
And I'm afraid my dearest darling Barb I can't let you retire
I need you here beside me each and every day
Without you I could not survive or live in any way
I just rely upon you as I have through married life
You've always been there for me my dearest darling wife
So please enjoy your birthday you are one of the best
I think I can allow you just one single day of rest
Report again for duty tomorrow when we'll see
The many ways that you can once more take good care of me.

7th. September 2007

# Your sixty fifth birthday.

Hi there my dear birthday girl, a special one this year
You've reached the age of sixty five but darling never fear
You're still a bit behind me with plenty of desire
It's time you took it easy and started to retire.
We've walked through life together for such a lot of years
We've faced so many problems and shed so many tears
It's time we slowed our lifestyle down and found more time somehow
To enjoy our hours together and let the children keep us now!
Let's treasure every moment as we share each passing day
We only need each other, true love in every way.
So Barb enjoy your birthday and never mind your age
Life offers many pleasures  throughout every stage
Let's have a drink or maybe two, it's time to celebrate
No matter what your age may be you'll always be my mate.

# 66th Birthday.

Another year has passed us by and what a year it's been,
 It's taken you to sixty six, I know you're not too keen
But you are still four years behind your husbands massive age
 Imagine when you're seventy, no need to throw a rage
These years can be exciting, there's lots of life left yet
 So let's enjoy each moment, no time to cry or fret.
We've even recently moved house to somewhere we both know
 And for the first time in our life we have a bungalow!
It really is a super place, our very own love nest
 And thanks to all the family it really is the best.
Our kids look after both of us, they make us feel so proud
 We want to sing their praises and shout our thanks out loud.
So let's have no more crying, life has just been great
 And we'll go on together, you'll always be my mate
A happy birthday darling, our love will never die
 My life is really now complete and you're the reason why
And what of you my darling, there's one thing I must say
 In forty years of married life I love you more each day
There's nothing I would rather do, nowhere I'd rather be
 Than by your side each night and day, you mean the world to me.

# Dearest daughter Denise.

We'd love to see you and Dean wed
 But it's hard to see so far ahead
When you're getting old and grey
 And facing problems every day.
Now we've heard there's a Wedding sale
 With a tiara and a certain veil
That you would love, or so they say
 To wear on your special day.
So we thought it must be time
 For us to act and give a dime
To help make you a happy bride
 And wear them both with love and pride.
Waste no more time, get on your way
And grab them both without delay.
Don't dare to argue, make no fuss
 Because you do so much for us
It is the least that we can do
 To show how much we both love you
And it makes us proud and very glad
 To call ourselves your mum and dad.

All our love always, darling.

# February 3rd. 2009

We've reached another milestone in our married life,
    Forty-one years ago was the day that you became my wife.
Do you remember that weekend and what a time we had
    At Yarmouth with the family and your dear Mum and Dad
Drinking in the Iron Duke, so many things to do,
    Those were exciting days when I fell in love with you.
'Twas the beginning of our story that's lasted all these years,
    We've had our happy moments and shared a few sad tears.
But overall it's been just great and three good kids to show,
    Every day from then and still I've always loved you so.
This last year has been difficult but my love has not run cold,
    There's some things we no longer do,truth is we're getting old.
We live our lives more slowly now, there's times that we have
    cried,
    But as we go on together we're always side by side.
I will never leave you Barb, what will be will be,
    My love will never falter for you mean the world to me.
As our health deteriorates, as it no doubt will do,
Nothing can dim the love I have for you.

That's it Barb, Happy Anniversary darling, all my love always,
    Len.

# A Summers Day.

Our life is like a Summers Day beginning with the dawn,
The beauty of the daybreak is the time when we were born
The morning is our childhood years, gay and so carefree
Nothing causes worry, no responsibility.
Then there is the hottest time all around midday
Represents our youthful years hard at work and play.
The breeze of early afternoon, the ever present sun
That's the middle part of life, our crazy years are done.
We settle down and build our life, we have a family,
Make our plans and choose just what our future is to be.
The later afternoon our children go off on their own
And leave the older generation at home all alone.
The quietness of the evening becomes our twilight years,
The shadows start to lengthen, our laughter turns to tears
Until the darkness settles in to take our life away
The night time will prepare us for an even brighter day.

# The Final Poem.

## A Life of Love.

The time has come to draw a close to the poems I've written for you,
 Our truly wonderful lifetime of love is very nearly through.
After I wrote the last one I found it hard to understand
 My life received a nasty shock when fate called and took a hand.
You were diagnosed with Alzeimers, a disease so cruel and sad
 It drove a wedge between our love and all the fun we'd had.
Well over a thousand words I've penned especially for you,
 I'd gladly write a thousand more if you'd understand a few
But your powers of observation and the precious gift of speech
 Both have sadly left you and are now well out of reach.
You're living in a silent world with normal feelings gone
 And yet you're never giving up, you just keep struggling on.
I see you every single day though you're in full time care
 I cry myself to sleep each night because you're never there.
I'm not looking for your sympathy for me or for my wife
 We've both been very lucky in a long and happy life,
Some people have no life at all or are cut down in their prime
 Victims of an accident or a cruel and hideous crime
So when the curtain closes and the call comes from above
 I pray we'll be together to share another lifetime of true love.

# Last word

(By Len Biddlecombe)

Now I have retired I have much more time to concentrate on my favourite hobby, the written word.

I enjoy writing poetry though my first love has to be short fictional stories on a wide variety of subjects. I have currently written over thirty and hope to have them published soon.

# Len Biddlecombe

Len has more than 40 short stories and a wealth of poetry. If you would like to be kept up to date with his publishing please visit

www.Blackheathdawn.co.uk

Or

www.Blackheathdawnwriters.co.uk/lenbiddlecombe

7733472R00039

Printed in Great Britain
by Amazon.co.uk, Ltd.,
Marston Gate.